THE PRODIGAL SON

Poems 1956–1959

THE
PRODIGAL SON

Poems 1956–1959
by
James Kirkup

LONDON
OXFORD UNIVERSITY PRESS
NEW YORK   TORONTO
1959

Oxford University Press, Amen House, London E.C.4

GLASGOW NEW YORK TORONTO MELBOURNE WELLINGTON
BOMBAY CALCUTTA MADRAS KARACHI KUALA LUMPUR
CAPE TOWN IBADAN NAIROBI ACCRA

PRINTED IN GREAT BRITAIN

ACKNOWLEDGEMENTS

ACKNOWLEDGEMENTS are made to the editors of the following periodicals in which some of these poems first appeared: *Moderna Språk* (Stockholm), *New Poems 1958, Eigoseinen* (Tokyo), *The Listener, The Times Literary Supplement, Bungei Ritsu* (Hokkaido), *The New Yorker, Image,* and *Time and Tide.*

CONTENTS

I

II

III

IV

V

viii

VI

VII

I

WAITING

I WAIT with a pencil in my hand
Beside the morning's empty page,
Not hoping for a sign, but waiting
For a word that will engage
The stillness with a sound
Of its own making.

Outside the paper room
The children in the playground kill
The summer with their cries.
I look out at the sunny hill
Of sky, but cannot catch the words they scream
To give their spirits ease.

If I, too, could give a shout
Of fear or pleasure, I could play
Myself into their endless game.
But I stand outside their day.
The dumb words are fastened in my throat,
And will not come.

THE SOLITARY POET

THIS paper is the face
Of one you hoped for most.
A word will take its place,
And lay that lonely ghost.

You cannot share a word
That will not give you rest.
Your longing is absurd.
To be alone is best.

Seek in the lonely view
A care for human kind.
No other word will do
But the one you cannot find.

THE LOST POEM

WILL what I now begin to write
Become the poem I have lost
So long, and did not wish
    To find again?

How can I know which way
My love's light thought has gone,
Or know if I may find
    His house again?

Somewhere there is a path he treads:
A certain light falls round his head.
He will not come to me, so I
    Must seek again.

Through a dark city running
I go, to find his window lighted;
But weep, seeing it unlit
    And lost again.

AFTER PENTECOST

THE wonder is that I write
This, when I cannot find a word.
Once everything came to my hand,
The farthest phrases, and the closest calls,
And I drew my meaning lightly
From the waters of a page.

I filled each line
With something more than words,
And kept the spirit moving
Like spring and summer, easily
As birds, or the shadow of wind in leaves
Over the waters of a page.

A bitter season
Of death and parting
Found the heart, that once
Was durable, done,
And the rippling gone
From the waters of a page.

—My fate is still unknown.
I cannot tell if I
Am well or ill;
The world is far away
That once I mirrored close
Upon the waters of a page.

Yet for the first time now,
As if I learned to speak
Again, after a long dumbness,
I seek the wind of a word.
The wonder is that I write
This, upon the waters of a page.

METAMORPHOSIS

IN the narrow boat of earth
Let me lie, and have my birth.
Let me with my final breath
Take that voyage into death
Over the mountains' rigid waves
And under the fountains' glassy graves,
Through the forests of the mine,
Along the furnace of the spine
And down the quarries of the bone
Into the atmospheres of stone.

There let my spirit's even keel
Rise upright on rocky heel.
Let the dark be such a night
As to call the eye to light.
—And let such dense a quiet be
That my tongue returns to me.

II

COWS

In buttercup and daisy fields
The lowing cattle, white and brown,
Lie by the creamy hedge of may,
Or up to their shoulders stand
In waves of clovered hay.

Under the pasture's trees that grow
Out of their own dark pools of green
They gather in the evening's pale
Summerhouse of sky and leaves,
And milk the shadows of the brindled vale.

A HOUSE IN SUMMER

In the dusk of garden fagged by the electric day,
Pale washing hung beyond the blackening roses
Shifts like restless visitors who cannot get away.
The blinding sun is clenched, as evening discomposes,
In dunderheaded clouds, that squeeze it out of sight.
Great trees are staggered by the merest breath of night.

All doors are open in the choking house,
And no one seems to know where anyone has gone:
All are at home, but absent; in, but out.
A person leans in a twilight corner like a gun,
Lighting his face with the last rays from a book
Whose leaves never stir, though he gives them look after
    look.

At an open window, a tree rustles, curiously close, its wood
Full of exhausted patience, patient still.
The window seems to take in much more than it should—
An entire garden, the lake beyond, a dog over a hill:
They are all inside the open house, like the air
Moved in from the afternoon, left hanging round the stair.

In the bedrooms, twilight cannot quite extinguish
The blank abandon of beds unmade by heat.
The morning's thrown-back coverings bloom and languish
Like knocked-out lovers under the ceiling's even sheet.
The attics throb like ovens and their stone tiles tick.
Baked books are warm still, their floury pages thick.

A door closes. Another. A window left open is no longer
    wide.
A looking-glass is blighted with its own vain repetitions:
Its dusty coolness draws the lost inhabitants inside.
—Faces dark with summer, they drift like apparitions,
Bringing each other the last of day, the first of night
In a wide room suddenly shuttered by unnatural light.

THE FALLING FLOWER

In the lamplight's vermilion shade
The dark red peony unfolds
Its hundred-petalled fans.
The fire's coral breath unloads
In a random shower
This quietly exploding rose.

Slowly the stillness
Lets handfuls of petals fall.
On the pink-checked tablecloth
Softly the flower pounces,
Weighing this dying hour
In its own crimson ounces.

THE LAKESIDE, CORSHAM

A STERN swan, his neck a question,
Swam to me out of the liquid sun
That lapped the listening water on
The wild talk of a quiet stone.
He appeared to listen at the lake's deep brim.

Long and alone in the dim
Undercover cavern of the leaves'
Reflecting, green-lapping eaves,
I leaned, over and under the moving waves.
Nothing was wearing the water's gloves.

Over the laketop's brilliant graves
A bird's note, like a stone knocking,
Was knocked on a stone, starting, stopping.
The tapping water fluttered with coupling
Lights on the sun-riddled leaves overlapping.

In washes of green over green overlapping
On nothing but evening melting the flake of the moon.
—Then in the darkling air of the lake's deep swoon,
Gravely pondered, swam serenely away with the sun
Of an answered question, silent, a swan.

EARLY RAIN

AFTER the long drought
The sun goes quickly out.
Leaf after leaf in the laden trees
Like cats' ears flick.
Dusty flowers on a dry stick
Stagger beneath the blows
Of the downpour breeze.
Each tree is a sounding drum,
And every rose
Is trampled in the hum
Of the shower's watery bees.

BLOOD punches through every vein
As lightning strips the windowpane.

Under its flashing whip, a white
Village leaps to light.

On tubs of thunder, fists of rain
Slog it out of sight again.

Blood punches the heart with fright
As rain belts the village night.

DOWNFIELD CROSSING HALT

I HEAR a drowning steeple
High and dry in tidy crops.
With the whack of a kitchen chopper
The signal drops.

A clock's blank dial, dazed
By a fringe of figures, tries
To puzzle things out. A frown
Threatens the keyhole eyes.

What does it mean, that stare
Of a village schoolboy bad at sums?
—The train is only slightly late,
But this answer never comes.

SUMMER NIGHT

As we walk, the moon ahead of us
Appears to be falling through
Each tree we pass, and sieves
Star after star through screens
Of thickening leaves.

The green hedge is wider now
With white may, hanging grass. The chestnut
Trims itself with pink and snowy cones;
The moon as we walk drops through each tree
And scatters silvery grit among the country stones.

POSY

A BUNCH of common flowers, held
As if in a child's hand
By a jar of crystal rain, resumes
The domestic summer, an offering
Selected from a wilder air
To give a muted greeting to the room.

Behind them, the lace curtain's repeated roses
Pattern the window-pane, and reach
The garden's primitive bouquet
To the world of wind and birds,
Where a green hedge, a hill of trees
Restore these natives to their habitat of leaves.

BIRD WATCHING

LYING in strong, deep-summer grass, we view
  A life of brief, perpetual dangers:
Eyes sharpened on beads of dew,
  Heads tilted at a world of strangers.

A witty flight transcends the pain
  Of death's mad tussle in the shade
For a breast speckled with dabs of rain,
  A nest love's neat intelligence has made.

Watch! All is not gentle here:
  Mating is fierce, fights are shrill.
Legs always flexed for flight,
  Anxiety has claws that kill.

Why can we never speak a word,
  Tell each other not to be afraid?
No human voice is terror to a bird,
  But we no longer speak the language of the glade.

THE FLY'S ETERNITY

The spider plots and tramples
    His sheer and knotted ways:
Upon the shivered window
    He strains a clearer maze.

Brave, with himself compacted,
    His tackle trim and tight,
He varnishes with nothing
    A pattern pegged on light.

His limits known, he ventures
    Infinity in a line,
And stretches, quick funambulist,
    A point however fine.

He makes a strength of weakness;
    Utility's an art.
Against the sun he tenses
    His passion's equal heart.

He casts upon the window
    His grim transparency,
Elaborates a rainbow,
    The fly's eternity.

IN A SAILPLANE

STILL as a bird
Transfixed in flight
We shiver and flow
Into leagues of light.

Rising and turning
Without a sound
As summer lifts us
Off the ground.

The sky's deep bell
Of glass rings down.
We slip in a sea
That cannot drown.

We kick the wide
Horizon's blues
Like a cluttering hoop
From round our shoes.

This easy 'plane
So quietly speaks,
Like a tree it sighs
In silvery shrieks.

Neatly we soar
Through a roaring cloud:
Its caverns of snow
Are dark and loud.

Into banks of sun
Above the drifts
Of quilted cloud
Our stillness shifts.

Here no curious
Bird comes near.
We float alone
In a snowman's sphere.

Higher than spires
Where breath is rare
We beat the shires
Of racing air.

Up the cliff
Of sheer no-place
We swarm a rope
That swings on space.

Breezed by a star's
Protracted stare
We watch the earth
Drop out of air.

Red stars of light
Burn on the round
Of land: street-constellations
Strew the ground.

Their bridges leap
From town to town:
Into lighted dusk
We circle down.

Still as a bird
Transfixed in flight
We come to nest
In the field of night.

HURDY GURDY

SMOOTHLY the handle turns
And turns, but still
The ballad trips and stumbles,
Lavishing its mad
Pauses and its fits
Of fancy in a neat
Shambles, a repeated waltz.

An entire springtime
Staggers its broken beat.
The antiquated tune,
A fistful of paper roses,
Sprinkles its thin
Pennies, and plays
The uneasy street.

THE ASTRONAUT

STAR-SAILOR, with your eyes on space,
You map an ocean in the sky at night.
I see you stride with scientific grace
Upon the crusted suns of yesterday
As if it were to-morrow, in the place
Of time, the voyager beyond this momentary stay
Whose loaded instruments of light
Shoot rocket-galaxies around the bend of sight.

In this world a tablecloth need not be laid
On any table, but is spread out anywhere
Upon the always equidistant and
Invisible legs of gravity's wild air.

The tea, which never would grow cold,
Gathers itself into a wet and steaming ball,
And hurls its liquid molecules at anybody's head,
Or dances, eternal bilboquet,
In and out of the suspended cups up-
Ended in the weightless hands
Of chronically nervous jerks
Who yet would never spill a drop,
Their mouths agape for passing cakes.

Lumps of sparkling sugar
Sling themselves out of their crystal bowl
With a disordered fountain's
Ornamental stops and starts.
The milk describes a permanent parabola
Girdled with satellites of spinning tarts.

The future lives with graciousness.
The hostess finds her problems eased,
For there is honey still for tea
And butter keeps the ceiling greased.

She will provide, of course,
No cake-forks, spoons or knives.
They are so sharp, so dangerously gadabout,
It is regarded as a social misdemeanour
To put them out.

THE CLOWN

Circo Price, Madrid

HE wears the spangled pantaloons
And swings their divided crinoline
From clever hips, where bitty rings
On blanched fingers point his quips.

A bracelet of brilliants round
One bony ankle coruscates
White stockings and pointed pumps
On slender shanks and tiny feet.

The dead-white face obliterates
All but the empty glitter of his eyes
And the thin red lips, like a tart's,
Rimming the dingy sparkle of a smile.

One huge black eyebrow, masked
In permanent inquiry, mocks
The other, significantly mean.
His questions beg the innocent reply.

His rustic companion's broad response
Is no concern of his, though he pretends surprise.
His smartness shames the heart, whose ignorance
Can ask no questions, and can tell no lies.

THE BODY-BUILDER

Temperamental as a prima donna, he
Clasps rugged fists upon his navel, and
Inflates the pecs for all to see.
A crowing cock will so expand.

Turning the back to spread his lats,
He struts a pose on sun-greased thighs.
He brags each inch of bicep, bats
Modest lids on self-appraising eyes.

One-hand snatches are his dreams,
Lifts, presses, pushes, jerks and swings,
Lateral raises, one-arm cleans.
Those double dumb-bells are his wings.

All deltoids, triceps and obliques,
Abdominals and well-placed meat,
Is the perfect torso that he seeks
Anatomically complete?

We look towards the face to find
The soul behind the pouch's pose.
What heavy handsomeness of mind
Instructs the proud set of his nose?

Is fitness a neurotic bore?
Does muscle-definition hide
A healthy vacancy, or more
Than what appears outside?

ALL-IN WRESTLERS

THESE two great men battling like lovers
Groan and pant in limbs that strangle,
Hold and abandon, clip and part.
Such is their longing for one another.
Each is the other's bitter angel,
Yet for love they wrestle, heart to heart.

They stand as close together
As those two young workmen, one of whom
Removes with the wetted corner of
His crumpled handkerchief a splinter
From his mate's left eye, a dumb
Show of man's concern for man, a silent love.

But then a leg is hooked, an arm once more
Is pressed beyond the limits of desire,
And one upon the other falls, who with a yell
Full of imploring anger beats the floor
With helpless fist, while his enemy, with cruel fire,
Grapples the loser to his breast, and screws him into hell.

III

SWEDISH EXERCISES

The Dead Falls at Ragunda

THIS was where a river fell away
And left a useless fall of stones.
Where once a mountain flashed
With rushing water hangs to-day
A still cataract of rock, dead bones
Of an elemental life whose waters crashed
And stumbled with ungovernable force,
While over the black pine forest clouds of spray
Marked the continuous thunders of its own applause.

Now where the waters fountained trees have sprung,
Among the boulders stained with spreading sores
And rings of lichen, silver birches leap
Like phantoms of the spray that hung
And shivered with the smoke of catastrophic wars.
—But the dead falls only seem to sleep.
Under their arrested avalanches lie
Ancestral heroes, gods of the epic north, whose tongue
Lingers among the stillnesses, and cannot die.

Ice-hockey in Dalarna

THE player's quilted shorts are red.
Padded shoulders and sweatered chest
    Appear to shrink that golden head.
He bears a different number from the rest.

    On booted skates he's tall.
Crimson stockings muscle knees and thighs
    And make his feet seem small.
Dark eyebrows draw a vizor on his eyes.

Over the open rink the forward leans and flies.
  He holds his stick in gauntlet clutch
And weaves the puck across the scoring ice.
  Like crabs the keepers in the goal-nets crouch.

Hard on the growling ice they thrust their blades,
  Scour the rink for danger and our rough delight.
Snow falls from the floodlights as the white sky fades,
  And captains shoot wet stars into the teeth of night.

In the Katarina Lift, Stockholm

THE ground drops, the street lamps fall away
With the speed of divers slowly hurtling through
The sluices of the deep, flyover dark.
Gradually, with a decent readiness,
The city like a bride unfolds herself,
Her willingness made modest by the night
That yet more fervently reveals her fire,
Those radiating centres of desire,
The clustered lights of crossings,
The jewelled veins of squares and parks,
The looped ropes of doubled radiance down the lakes
On which the golden ferries burn
And move like hands intelligently down
The swan-clouded currents in the knocking ice
Whose opening and closing estuaries finally reflect
A distant fall of houses, every window bright.

Now, at the tower's top, and in the hanging
Gondola of stars we stand astride
The city of our admiration, she who lies
Profuse, and naked, passionate yet calm,
Inscrutably collected, in a brilliant pause
Before the swoop of love, the fall without a cause.

Gymnasium

THE snowboots and the skis, the fur-lined hoods
That populate the coat-racks by the classroom door
Prepare me for an audience whose moods
Are those of warm relief and cold anxiety.
They have escaped the sharpness of the world outside.
Soon they must penetrate once more
The cruel street of ice, begin the homeward ride,
The battle with the snow, the wind's perplexity.

But for a moment all is warmth and light.
Pale-golden faces smile and laugh for me.
Their lips are pale, their perfect eyes are bright.
These boys are men with voices like the sea's.
Under the fragile desks their limbs are large,
Their laughter springs from huge
Good-nature that no winter night can freeze.
They are the giants of the forests that are men
Where legendary heroes lift their blond and massive heads
    again:
In their enormous hands a book
Tenderly flutters like captive birds,
And in their northern calmness is a generous look
Of level passion, stronger than any words.

Umeå

IN the park emptied by winter
I tread the undistinguished paths of snow and dark.
The pale bandstand adrift on scrolls
Of wind-turned music, and the metal baskets
Packed with the overflowing wastes of snow
Are frozen ghosts of unimaginable summers.

A piled church warms the sky with orange brick.
The river shuffles neon alphabets of acid green.
—I do not care where paths begin and borders end,
But in the naked birch-grove that I saunter through
The snow's calm anarchy keeps off the grass
My steps that go where no one else has been.

Jämtland

THE silver birch is papery, and veils
Its elbowed branches gloved with black
In a suspended shower of golden scales,
Its own slight leaves, that pattern a forest track
Like narrow starshine's riddled flakes
Or coins struck from the moonlight's hidden lakes.

A river is violet beneath the deep red clouds of dark.
The ash and aspen brandish sheaves
Of fireworks, each leaf a spark,
Along the forest's evergreen black eaves.
Rafts of logs lie on the sunset like an archipelago.
Mountains, pitched with pine, hang in the reeds below.

A green swan slings himself across the vacant air.
His rippling neck hauls on his feathered vanes.
Beyond the rowan drugged with berries, there
In a yellow sky along the lake he drags the water's reins,
Making the sheeted mirror flash and shake.
The washed reeds bow to the long processions of his wake.

He sails now among impenetrable mountains furred with
   larch,
Floats through the lake-reflected rainbow's double hoop
That frames the northern lightnings in its melting arch,
And over his own stern image seems to prowl and stoop;
While rosy distances of ice that draw him on
Still shiver through the birch-tree's page when he has gone.

34

IV

For if anything in the world is desirable, so
desirable that even the dull and brutish herd
would, in its more reflective moments, prize it
above silver and gold, it is that a ray of light
should fall on the darkness of our being, and that
we should come by some explanation of our
mysterious existence where nothing is clear but
its wretchedness and futility. But even if this
were attainable in itself, it is made impossible by
the compulsory solutions that are forced upon us.

CAMERA OBSCURA

A LIGHT will fall
Upon the darkness of being
And it will show us
What is beyond seeing.

Sight is so small.
The sky is contracted
Through a shrinking lens,
And on a void refracted.

A lens of fear
Gripping the highest heavens
Plays on the screen of self
That blurs and deadens.

True space is beyond
The meaning of its only word,
Yet it comprehends
Thought's voiceless bird.

The skies remain.
Love, too, is there.
Life is a vision
Death can not out-stare.

LIGHT

A CANDLE stump is all
That is left of one
That was so tall.
But it keeps still
The feathered sun
A wick's white quill
Is trimmed upon.

The real end
Is not in sight,
But we befriend
This final stand
That lets our night,
A rose of wax, expand
Into a taller light.

THE GUIDING GHOST

STRICT and easy is that way,
Common to all, and yet most rare.
It is both serious and gay,
Narrow as waters, wide as air.

Though we are never soon or late,
It will attend each stop and start;
Yet runs, and does not hesitate,
Knowing the distance of each heart.

Secret, it lets the open way
Become both ours and its own.
However lost, we cannot stray,
Conducted, though we walk alone.

Our ghostly guide, the life we lead,
From body's want and spirit's pride
Distils the realities we need:
Through indecisions we decide.

THE TRUTH

THE empty laugh
Betrays a troubled mind,
The bitter smile
A soul that's blind.

The rigid spirit
Shows a face of stone.
Spite and anger
Consume the living bone.

A loud word
Is the body's lie.
A word abused
Will make men die.

Truth alone
Turns night to day.
Only the truth
Is truly gay.

THE NATURE OF LOVE

THE sun, God's eye,
Is infinite, its rays
Ungraspable, except
By a sharpened gaze.

Its love is all.
Yet we must give our sight
To convert a fraction
Of its open light.

Only the heart that makes
A prism of its doubt
Can split the infinite of light
That shutters nothing out.

GIVING AND TAKING

TAKE as a gift ·
A love all freely given.
A great Lord commends your thrift.
Keep as His gift
This hope of heaven.

To take is hard
For minds narrowed by living.
But open your breath to a word.
To take is hard,
When it is giving.

Let breath increase
Within your heart and spirit.
Your gain is His, His gain your lease
Of breath's increase
That gives life credit.

Faith is His bond
Love's capital assures.
Such grace does more than lend.
Faith is your bond.
Give. It is yours.

Give as a gift
A love all freely given.
A great word reveals its drift.
Treasure the gift
Of spendthrift heaven.

ACTORS AND PROMPTERS

THE landscape is created, and describes itself
Completely, yet the transforming eye
Selects what it requires, and constructs,
Out of the only possible landscape, one
That is also true. It takes what it desires to know
From what is given and can be perceived.

Eyes are capable of every ignorance.
But this eye does not want to use
What it ignores. Enough
Is not too much: using the bare bones
Of light's firm architecture, it decides
The colours and the shapes that must be there.

It does not take each leaf, but
One, a certain green among the many,
Yet that holds them all.
Shadows are not black, rivers not wholly white.
And always it remembers there are other eyes
That see another landscape, the same as this.

The lay of the land
Can be deceptive, though it is always right.
The line between sky and hill, like light and shade,
Is always changing, yet remains the same.
The eyes are actors; light is the prompter who
Tells them what they have to do.

THE INCREDIBLE THINKING MAN

I THINK, and every thought
Destroys me, a logical fate.
I work, and energy renews,
At its own expense, the task I hate.

I write, and the moment also
Writes itself off, another death.
I speak, and the time it takes
Is all of life to that one breath.

I live, and the incredible illusion
Perpetuates itself, but leaves no mark.
Die, and vanish permanently down
Indifferent and thoughtless dark.

V

Time steals our love,
And unalarmed,
Like untold treasure
Takes it openly away . . .

COMMON LOVE

BESIDE themselves with love,
Two faces resemble one another.
Equal portraits of a single grace,
They share a certain close regard,
A mask they openly assume to make
Their difference a parallel concern.

Still the demanding day
Reflects itself with interest behind
Their thought's compounded gazes.
Alone together, their opposing mirrors fuse
One likeness from infinities,
A profile echoed in the coin of love.

Its ring is true, its worth is more
Than coupled breathing, or the midnight's
Tangled treasures in the hold of sleep.
Self-sharers, in this liberal exchange
They secretly surrender the untouched reserves
That common love both squanders and preserves.

EXCHANGE OF PHOTOGRAPHS

In a park of empty flowerbeds
The sun splits boulders,
Taps testing hammers on our heads.

The sorry past still smoulders:
Here is the summer's friend, who shades his brow.
Another on last year's beaches oils his shoulders.

We do not seem to know them now.
There is no call to speak their names.
We pass on quickly, though we don't know how,

To someone's children, a family good at games,
The views from windows of obscure hotels,
The failures, self-deceits and shames,

The shabby longings and the awful sells.
—Indifferently we throw away
The torn faces of our several hells,

The unlearnt lessons we can say
By heart: all those are finished things.
Only this present love has come to stay.

Or has it?—Out of a score of poisoned Springs
We save two pictures, of ourselves, for luck,
And hurriedly exchange them, wishing they were rings.

CORDOBA

UNDER the noon's white walls
Where steep shadow piles its shade
A dry guitar
Sprinkles the courtyard air
With the complaint that love has made,
The steady hunger
Of the long unsatisfied,
The lonely lover
Clinging to the bars of pride.

SUITE SALMANTINA

*

AT five of the stars I wake
On a rare October morning,
And a poem overflows
My candid dark.

I keep my eyes closed,
Happy, pretending sleep,
With a gift in my head for you,
Another in my heart.

Suddenly both are one.
I am writing with open eyes
The words I dreamt for you,
As if the familiar were new.

The paper warms to them
And to my flowing hand
With the untidy fire
Of the bed I burned to leave.

Looking to where the dark
Shelters the house in which you lie,
I feel my heart beat like a boy's
On Christmas morning, in a house of toys.

*

Each day now is Christmas,
With the present of the day before
Still with me, past being broken,
And the present day's own gift
Still to be given and received.

Love gives each morning's air,
Cleansed by the sun's wide sweeps of blue,
A breath of celebration, spicy
As the wind-thrown fragrance of your hair,
The very essence that is only you.

*

Your eyes first looked into these words
With that steady honesty you give
To cats and ballads, food and birds,
To fields and faces, sticks and stones,
And only then they seemed to live:
I felt your body in my flesh and bones.

*

I dream of you asleep:
A contained sweetness,
Warm, and full, and deep.

I think of your completeness,
And the way you place
A gentle strength, a neatness

In a line that orders grace
With wildness; the unexpected break
Of phrase that lights your face,

The seaman's eyes that shake
Their pale blue fires on the prow
Of poetry, your sparkling wake.

*

True love alone can write
Because it asks no more
Than its undemanding light
To burn out passion's core
Of self, with care for others' sight.

A pure flame burns my snow.
I melt and freeze,
But I am water, too, and flow,
To give my driven spirit ease,
In a single tear, that is the joy I know.

My hand runs like a delta through
These maps my soundings make.
Although I draw them all for you,
And keep a lighthouse for your sake,
All men may use them, for my love is true.

*

Love blinds, but makes me see
Life's folly clear as day.
My self has gone away from me
And nothing come to stay.
Only the love I flee
Is true, and will not go away.

*

Instead of a despair, believe
True love is never lost.
Though no hand will receive
Its foolish gift, its ghost
Will not go wandering without release
Along the rivers of the midnight air.

Although the body finds no peace,
True love is in the spirit's care,
And is not wasted in a selfish sigh.
—This one truth I find in you
Is gathered by the waters and the sky,
And is not lost, because my love is true.

*

I seem to hear you stir, as if
You were only in the other room.
Distance has paper walls.
The air between us
Is your breath and mine.

Though you are close,
You are most far away.
But because you are so dear
I bring you through the paper wall
That is neither there, nor here.

*

You are the only ghost
I ever truly loved,
Because your presence moved
My heart with more than lust.

With not a single touch
And with no human kiss
You brought my life to this
Wild calm that holds so much.

Not only gaiety and trust
I learnt from your repose,
But that true passion grows,
Like art, because it must.

53

O, with a single look
I felt the darkness change.
And it was nothing strange:
The opening of a book.

In the brightness of the sun
You bring a moonlit air.
No ghost had ever gifts as rare,
Or love more substance, than this only one.

*

The dawn strikes up its music in the dark.
Behind the black cathedrals of the square
Cocks shout, and wake the grumbling dogs.
Great domes compose their masses on the air.

A flock of doves, cast from the breeze's hand,
Crockets a pinnacle with wings on wings.
Bells beat at the morning stars like fans,
And in between their silence rings.

Street-lamps still illuminate
Each level, long façade.
But the roofs' inventive arabesques
Are black against a shell of jade.

Translucencies are brushed with clouds
And furred with feathers, with the bloom
Of dark and fronded trees.
The city breathes, and flows into my room.

I lean from a window like a statue from a wall,
And dip my face into the fountains of the east.
A chimney slowly hangs out smoke.
My eyes are brimmed with the horizon's feast.

Now jade is blue: grey distances are slashed with red.
The fretted spires are pierced with white.
—I look towards these preparations for the sun,
And see your face lift from its dream of night.

*

I wait for the drown
Of evening, when we go,
Together and together, through
The sinking town,
A meeting that is not a rendezvous
With loneliness and dark,
And stiff knives thicketing a naked park.

Slowly the roofs go down,
Releasing buoyant stars
To mark the watered sky with spars
Of light, a splintering crown
That binds our hidden scars
With stone, and keeps our heads above
The wrecks of solitude and love.

*

Wandering alone at midnight
Along the streets we walked together,
I was a stranger once again,
For everything was unfamiliar,
Changed by the loneliness as much
As by your presence at my side.

Even the stars were altered.
The fixed positions that I saw with you
Now seemed obscure.
I could not find my orient,
Or the pole that keeps its compass in your hand
At meeting and at parting, night and day.

Then I found myself beneath
Your window lighted from within,
And for a moment watched
Your shadow move across the glass.
I gave a shout: but as I looked,
Even that last star went out.

*

Now you are waking to our common air
That is the same for sleepers and their mates,
For those who watch and wonder at the rare
Bright morning that combines our separate fates.

Let this long day be full for you,
Filled with your working sun
That makes the heavens white and blue
Above the brown horizons where your poems run.

*

Salamanca,
October, 1957

56

BY THE TORMES

THE first star, liquid Sirius,
Drips in the river's glass its slender
Chandelier. Its lustre, long as light,
Drops brimming candles deep
Into the melting mirrors of the night.

A swimming creature undulates the sky, and shakes
The limpid evening to a pulse of cool desire,
A weeping star that mends itself in time
With lost light that trembles round
The bend of space, and barely breaks.

RECUERDO DE SALAMANCA

THE rain beats on the window
As the bells beat down the dark.
I wonder where you are, and if
You walk in rain, or under stars.

The bells beat into my memory
The days and nights we knew
In this one room, under the city's
Panoplies of stone. And so to you

I send this whispered message
Through the fastnesses of wind and rain—
To you, whose face begins to fade
Till only the hidden bones remain:

Stay true to our belief
In one another and our singular art.
If the rain beats for me, it beats
For both of us. I hear it falling in your heart.

FESTIVAL TAURINO: CIUDAD RODRIGO

Under the square's deep bell of sun
That hammers rings of faces round
The rough arena carpentered with cries,
A battered music has begun.

Ten swanking matadors
Parade the holy ground
Where truth indifferently is killed.
—The peasant springtime sweats and roars,
While the saint of Christ in dusty skies
Smiles on the murder love has willed,
And innocence in blood is bravely drowned.

SMOKE IN SUNLIGHT

In a thin shaft of winter sun
That folds the promise of an afternoon
Into the hothouse of my empty room,
The smoke from an idle cigarette is snatched
And curdled like a thread of milk
In water, twists a scarf of flowered chalk
Whose pattern curls and stretches
Along the naked arm of light
And draws itself across the window, whose iron grille
In a last, slow gesture patiently dissolves
These misty fires, tears to shreds of dust
My pictured breath, the lovely coil
Of life, the image of a death.

VI

SEVEN PICTURES FROM CHINA

I. *Dragonflies*

by HUANG SHEN

THEY hover on the page
And print themselves in ink
That makes a shadow of their wings
And weights their bodies on their longshanks'
Weightless springs.

The stalk of corn
Hardly bends beneath
Their flight. Its dry ear
Is heavier than those dragons
Of the air, that live on light.

II. *Lady with a Fan*

by FEI TAU HSÜ

THERE is a flower
Or a jewel in
Your looped-back hair,
And you stand, in a white
Robe that takes your pose,
Before a little fence
No higher than a flower:
Its two bars and
A single stick
Suggest a precipice.

There are wet grasses at your feet,
And above you the bare
Willow is weeping into
Nothing, the paper's mist.

Why do you lean there
Against a mossy rock,
And turn your quiet face away
Into your fan's white air?

III. *Mountain Landscape*

by TAI PÉN-HSAIO

SEEN as if
From a great height,
The fantastic clifftop
Is level with our eyes.

Its tops and terraces
Are bare, or furred
With pines. Distances
Are stacked in mist.

Beneath us, in a dark
Ravine cascading
Recent rains,
The trees are wild.

There is a bridge that leads
From rocks to stones;
And in a windy summerhouse
Among bamboos, two friends
Are where the bandit landscape
Both begins and ends.

64

iv. *Blossom*

by CHU TA

THE plum tree's leaves
Are brushed across
The wet page
Until they bloom
Their soft darkness
Into a space
Of mist
Whose emptiness unfolds,
Scented by the brush,
A flower,
Single, the first
Upon the Spring's
Bare pencil of a bough.

v. *Landscape*

by CH'ÊNG SUI

FROM a mountainside,
We look dizzily down
Through an ancient willow.

Across the bay
The peninsulas of rocks and trees
Fan the mist away
Into a poem on
A last inch of sky,
Indelible horizon.

In a narrow boat,
Curved and shallow as a leaf,
A lady and her boatman float
Upon the mist that hangs
Under and over their watery way.

She sits, with her white
Face lighting her black hair,
In the pale robe of ceremony.

The boatman in a pointed hat
Poles with dark hands
Their fragile craft
Towards a distant shore,
Where, set in a dry cliff among
Dark pines, a little house invents

A figure watching from an upper window
A dry leaf drifting on the misty bay.

VI. *Flowers*

by HUANG SHEN

YOU who were known as one
Of the eight eccentric painters of Yangchow
Have taken ink
And turned it to a flower
Balanced like a bird upon
The scribbled poem's
Watery alphabet of song.

VII. *Autumn Grove after Rain*

by WEN TIEN

ADRIFT in space,
The mountain's bare outline,
And a lower mountain's

Rocky waterfall—a white
Cleft on white mist—
With here a few
Slopes of pines,
And there a fall
Of mossy stones
That tumble soundlessly
Into a whiteness
That is either lake
Or sea or mist,
Or nothing—

On which a grove of trees
Floats away on flat rocks,
With a thatched summerhouse
And a tiny man
Fishing
From only
Half a bridge

TWO PICTURES FROM JAPAN

I. *The Bamboo Grove in Rain*

THE bamboo grove is flickering like rain
That touches with every drop
Each leaf on every jointed cane.

High in the pattered blades
A spired temple tops its thatch.
Below, in the dripping glades,

Two men in the pale
Dusk are tiny as they lead
Two donkeys down a misty bamboo-trail.

II. *All and Nothing*

IN the mist of the paper
Two boats leave a single ripple.
They are very small.

High in a far
Corner of the air, a peak
Hangs on nothing. That is all.

LONDON—TOKYO

THERE is no other creature like
The one fate sets beside us in a 'plane:
The vivacious grandmother, experienced traveller;
The amateur technician—'Don't look now, but
That number four propeller seems to be fluctuating
    madly—';
The convent schoolgirl mooning over Simone Weil;
The Indian mystic with his blissful flies undone;
The British maniac scribbling postcards all the night,
Counting and re-counting his collected works
That he stacks and shuffles, deals like decks of cards.

However wild a silence we may keep,
We moodily involve them in our private glooms:
We turn their glance upon the old moon lying on its back,
And wolf their breakfasts on our individual trays.
He knows 'the little boys' room' at every gritty port,
While she, 'at crazy prices,' snaps up fags and lipsticks,
    drink and scent.

Reaching their several destinations, they
Matily wish us 'Happy Landings!' while we try
To smile blandly as the shuddering jet-plane takes
Its running jump at yet another sky.

JAPANESE CHILDREN

THE round, calm faces rosy with the cold
Are squared by a window of black hair
From which the delicate features peep:
Eyes dark sloes that slide in sleepy lids,
The happy nose, lips plump as robins.

Grave, cosy dolls in their padded clothes,
Patiently they stand in the swimming snow
Beside mother and father, quiet and good.
On the mother's back, wrapped warm inside her flowered
    cape,
The fat, drowsy baby blinks, and does not cry.

THE VISITING CARD

To ATSUO KOBAYASHI, *who designed it*

THIS formal introduction is my first,
Most necessary purchase in Japan.
I who in England
Never pay visits
And rarely receive them
Here must provide myself
With the visitor's passport:
My name, status and address—
33, Kozenji-dori, the street
Of the name of a temple—
Are neatly inscribed in italic Romaji.
One hundred cards in this little box:
A lifetime of meetings in a single place.

But—turn the card over—what is this?
A witty flickering of strokes, like
The crossed leaves of a bamboo grove,
Lively, spattered with sun and rain,
Or the bird-printed corners of smiling eyes,
These small, quick signs
Translate my name and status,
And—if my learned colleagues will forgive me
For so calling it—my 'business' address.
—And in even smaller characters,
Like a picture-poem's miniature cascade,
There hangs beside it, in the card's white mist,
33, Kozenji-dori, Sendai.

SAKUNAMI

In the city of Sendai, electric cold
Loudspeakers the crowded pavements
While snow stills the falling dusk
And shrouds the streets with freezing flags.

In the packed bus that sharply draws
The widening country round our eyes
The men are talking Saturday talk,
The girls smile with Sunday smiles.

In village gardens, snow
Caps all the straw-trussed trees;
The landscape's calligraphy unrolls
Its long winter picture's endless dreams.

Red-cheeked country children trot
And paddle in the turning snow:
Old women in dark clothes
Bear striped bundles down deep white lanes.

Wild workmen stamp their muffled clogs,
Blow tufts of steam into the churning air,
And in their bristling capes of reeds
Like porcupines plunge through a hedge of flakes.

At Shirasawa, the narrow bridges turn
To snowdrifts over rocky streams,
And the conductor goes with a red flag
In the dramatic headlamps, to show the way.

Through the grey twilight, mountains
Hump their shaggy backs like camels.
The village shops are caves of fruit and toys;
On curved roofs, dark tiles are muffed with white.

Deep in the mountainous night
The lamps of Sakunami bleach the snow.
The mats in the sliding rooms are cool,
The pale rice-wine as warm as kisses.

The long bath grills us to the bone.
At Roman ease, up to the neck we lie
In hot spring-water from the boiling
Cauldrons of the earth, while candid snow,

A midwinter midnight's dream,
Flowers black boughs and green bamboos
With clumps of crystal, paper leaves
Beyond the ice-fringed windows of the bath.

In the cool-screened room the brazier glows:
Low lantern-light: soup steams: fresh oysters
Grey and silver in a white bowl
Of lemon chrysanthemum-petals.

We sleep on the floor in the house of wood
That creaks gently while the snow
Glides silently outside, like ghosts
Wandering houseless from suspended waterfalls of ice.

In the new morning at Sakunami
I sip a bowl of fragrant tea, feeling a quiet joy
As I watch from the floor of our tranquil room
The mountains soundlessly rising in the falling snow.

WRONG NUMBER

In the dead middle of the night,
Like a bad alarm-clock
The telephone shook me awake,
And from a long dream I jumped
Right out of my skin, afraid
To hear sad news of you.

Instead, I heard, still half-asleep,
The smoky music of a bar,
A man's voice faintly singing, and then,
As if she were at my side,
A woman repeating a question
In a language I cannot understand.

All I could answer was: Hullo? Hullo?
And she, alarmed, cried: Mashi mashi?
Astounded to hear her friend speak English.
Then she uttered a cry like a bird
In a voice still pretty with surprise, and,
As if I'd given her an electric shock, rang off.

The bar, the music and the voices vanished,
And left me alone again. Returning to bed
In the dead middle of the night
I peeped out at my snowy garden,
And was suddenly glad to be alone, and sober,
At home, with no sad news of you.

MUSIC AT THE SILVER STAR
COFFEE BAR, SENDAI

OUT of the street's sunny cold
We enter a warm, dim cave;
On the dark blue walls
A few muted lamps are hung.

Here is the mysterious quiet
Of a temple, where the worshippers
Sit listening with half-closed eyes
To music from another world.

The faint, bird-like conversations,
Like the record's hiss, are immaterial.
The classical concerto sings again
Its sharp, sweet, melancholy phrases.

I who have been so long indifferent to its grace
In this far country find my music restored to me, and
    cannot speak
As my dry heart drinks its native rain
And a long tear slowly lights my cheek.

WINTER INVITATION TO SPRING
IN KYOTO

In my house of paper
I glide on the matted floors,
Catching the wide sleeves of my tanzen
In all the sliding doors.

On the straw mats reclining
By the low table, I suspend
My hand's transparent fan above
The charcoal brazier, wishing for a friend.

The windows' glazed divisions
Let in the light of snow,
And the wet glint of an icicle,
A bare and crusted bough.

The tea will be faint green
In the dolls' cups of a tender blue.
—Until the bare branch is snowed
With blossom, I shall wish for you.

EARTHQUAKE

An old man's flamingo-coloured kite
Twitches higher over tiled roofs.
Idly gazing through the metal gauze
That nets the winter sun beyond my sliding windows,
I notice that all the telegraph-poles along the lane
Are waggling convulsively, and the wires
Bounce like skipping-ropes round flustered birds.
The earth creeps under the floor. A cherry tree
Agitates itself outside, but it is no wind
That makes the long bamboo palisade
Begin to undulate down all its length.

The clock stammers and stops. There is a queer racket,
Like someone rapping on the wooden walls,
Then through the ceiling's falling flakes I see
The brass handles on a high chest of drawers
Dithering and dancing in a brisk distraction.
The lamp swings like a headache, and the whole house
Rotates slightly on grinding rollers.
Smoothly, like a spoilt child putting out a tongue,
A drawer shoots half-out, and quietly glides back again,
Closed with a snap of teeth, a sharper click
Than such a casual grimace prepared me for.

The stove-pipe's awkward elbow
Twangles its three supporting wires. Doors
Slam, fly open: my quiet maid erupts from
Nowhere, blushing furiously, yet smiling wildly
As if to explain, excuse, console and warn.
Together, like lost children in a fairy-tale
Who escape from an enchanter's evil cottage,
We rush out into the slightly unbalanced garden. A pole
Vibrates still like a plucked bass string,
But the ground no longer squirms beneath our feet,
And the trees are composing themselves, have birds again.

In the spooky quiet, a 'plane drones
Like a metal top, and though the sound
Gives a sense of disaster averted,
And is even oddly re-assuring, as
The pulse of confident engines,
Throbbing high above an electric storm, can comfort,
We feel that somewhere out of sight
Something has done its worst. Meanwhile,
The house tries to look as if nothing had happened,
And over the roof's subtle curves
Lets the flamingo-coloured kite fly undisturbed.

ON A TANKA BY OCHI-AI NAOBUMI

You said that if only you could find
One man who would let himself be touched
By your poems, then you would die happy.

I have come too late to tell you
How your brief poem moved me
With its modesty and longing.

FOR A JAPANESE LADY'S FAN

To HITOSHI MIYANO

OUR hands flutter together
Over the embers in a brazier
Like two pale butterflies over
Deep red roses, never
Touching one another.

While they play and hover,
If they fan one finger
Tip against the other
Our hands will fall together
Into the roses' dying embers.

Fresh thorns will sting the clever
Hands that fly too close together
And fan each other
Into fire-petals over
Rose-embers of a sleeping treasure.

YIN AND YANG

THE circle is contained
Within itself, completes
A solitude. One heart
Within the other beats.

Two shapes connected
Become one lover
In a mingling glass.
Two ends consume each other.

White and blue are one:
They swim and turn together
Head to tail to head,
Ever, and for ever.

SOME COMMENTS ON YEATS'S 'AMONG SCHOOL CHILDREN'

For my students at Tohoku University

THE great-rooted poem, without wanting to do so,
Makes us one with you at the end,
Where, in an accelerando of
Questions, myths and invocations,
You become the new Pythagoras, or rather,
In becoming go beyond yourself, and him,
As the mother goes beyond herself in giving birth,
As child and mother go beyond themselves
In the genesis of recollection's honeyed sleeps,
And the dancer dancing out of his shadow leaps.

You become world-famous, in a world
Larger than that of the Ancients,
Where to be world-famous
One only needed to be known
In Rome or Athens. Nor is it world-famous
In the sense of the popular idol, but rather
Adding to the fame of earth.
—Then the smiling public man is truly public,
Creation's senator, no longer giving the official smile,
But, like a child again, in the momentary wonder,
Part accident, part knowing where to look,
Of copulation's glance and love's erratic mimicry,
You sit at last like her among the school-children,
Raising your hand, or hers, in invocation,
And asking, at the climax, question after question.

GEISHA DANCING

To KATSURA *at the Toyo Kan*

To the small music of a samisen,
Balancing your pale face and lacquered wig
Like too-heavy burdens on your child's thin neck,
You gently stamp your attitudes,
Working the air with an orange fan
That the orange lining of your sleeves
Echoes, an occasional surprise.

Your ribbed fan beats the drum of air,
Half-closes, and is stretched
Open by a finger-tip, so,
Like a bird's translucent wing
Whose springy feathers softly clatter,
Flash across your face's quiet moon,
The oblique eyes of a petted cat.

I sit and watch the mask of your face,
Trying to read in it again
The message you gave me with your eyes
When you knelt before me to serve the wine,
But find now no answering glance.
Your blank-powdered face compels me
To watch only the movements of the dance.

SNOWFALL ON MATSUSHIMA

FROM Shiogama roadstead, the distant islands look like
  sinking wrecks.
I sit on the straw mats of the boat, my eyes
Almost level with the water that the snow quietly plucks.
In wide sea-plantations, bamboo poles bear hammocks of
  weed.

Like castaways waving twisted branches from disintegrat-
  ing rafts,
The islands glide nearer, pass us one by one.
Their eroded shores are concave cliffs, that overhang
Like giant mushroom-caps pale stalks of stone.

Archways and tunnels are hung with veils of falling flakes.
Each crippled tree is plastered white, its branches shelves
  of snow.
Curtains of grey and amber icicles conceal
The caves, drifted with images, where masters meditated
  long ago.

Still the snow hauls its endless nets across the sea.
Their breaking meshes cannot hold the waters of the bay.
Nor can the sky's grey shoals of cloud be caught
In their own profusion, that casts and casts itself away.

POEM TO BE INSCRIBED ON A
JAPANESE KITE

FINDER, wherever I fall, that place
Is the one I hoped for; whether it be
On factory or temple roof or field of rice,
On Matsushima's islands or the Inland Sea,
On snowy mountain-flank or in the lee
Of the fisherman's boat, within the riven
Shadow of his leaning sail, I see
Your finder's hand draw up my kite to heaven
As if, from the endlessness of space,
You chose before all others my peculiar face,
And translated from a quiet star
Into your own wild tongue
These words with which I launch the air
And that the wind carries without care
To you, finder, like a falling song.

NOTES ON A POEM TO BE DROPPED
OUT OF AN UPPER WINDOW

INTO the falling snow
Another falling flake
Falls to the street below.

There I hear it break
Into laughter, tears, or a slow
Curse: each one is a mistake.

Better not to know
The sense its readers make.
Care only for the falling flake.

INVITATION TO A JAPANESE DOLL

COME, sit beside me on the floor
Beside the warm stone brazier.
There let us talk and make poems,
Look long at a flower together,
Listen to the cool sweep of the snow outside,
Drink wine, and sing, and fall happily silent
As we share the same cushion in the dusk,
And think the same thought.

KOKESHI KOKESHI

To HARUE OF SENDAI, *who painted it for me*

DOLL, my primitive pet,
I look into your painted face
With its nose slim as a flower stalk,
Its mouth neat as the bud
Of a red-tipped daisy,
And wonder what your eyes,
Those dark pools under your gently-sweeping lids,
See in my pale blue gaze.

The red flowers, freshly painted by a swift
And clever hand, the brush of Spring,
Adorn your body's naked bough
Like a new kimono, perfectly fitting.
—Doll, my primitive pet,
I stroke the shining fringe of your hair,
And lay my hand among your flowers
To find the wood's heart, their secret festival.

THE DREAM APART

In days funny with the drug, I dream,
Cleversides, of stages high as a precipice
Whose curtain of willing fireworks explodes
In a single acrobat, a clown, a spangled artifice.

He turns into three slow flamingos
That mount three perches as if he
Were one—(they are, he is)—and with the crack
Of a dislocated fan, smiles hard at me.

Opening the tinselled drama of his thighs,
He shows me the mauve lozenge of a heart
Like a sucked flower, warm
With the drug of meat, the dream apart.

CORRESPONDENCES

TODAY a letter from America—
From one of those professional
'Admirers of, and readers of,
And followers and indeed students of
Most all you've given us from your pen'—
A letter like a graduation exercise
From a course in creative appreciation
Of the art poem, how
To set about it, write
The thing and, naturally,
Market it: a letter
Asking with studied informality—
'On Xian-name terms
With most of your group'—
(First time I'd heard of it:
Always imagined, bud,
I was one on my own, way
Out on a limb, if you ask me,
No sense of community values either)—
And with the constant threat
Of a healthy smile in his
Goodguy's suntan, demanding,
With no shadow—'the world's a friendly place,
Really'—of ever being refused,
And making no mention of 'remuneration'—poets
Are known to be above all that,
Conveniently so for you, my
Tan-faced all-American boy, studying
'Comparative literatures of the world'—
(I seem to have heard that lark before)—
Well, it's one way, I guess,
Of getting to see Europe, though
'I never did get around
To seeing your Stratford, Worcestershire'—

And one day maybe you'll get around
To seeing Asia and the hoax
You try to play on old Japan, land of,
Who smiles, and plays along with you.
(But you, inflexible manipulator,
Could never play along with her,
Which is where she has you, kid,
Caught by the cock but not—how could you be—
By the imagination)—Yes,
Ever so casually, in
A letter signed 'Sincerely'—
(The 'meaningful experience' of
Your plastic handshake, rotary
As your anticipatory tourist beam
Of lucky-strike familiarity with
'Our good neighbour, the World')—
Where was I? Oh, yes, quietly
Giving me the invite, sir,
To send you 'any old
Drafts of poems'—particularly
On old laundry bills—(do poets have
Laundry?)—which literary critics tell us in
The authoritative biography, the poet always,
In fact, invariably
Utilized—'or any old stuff like that, any old
Rags I mean work-sheets, doodles, dribs,
Drabs or (quietly) hell, what-have-you.'

So much emerges.
After such conditioning,
My response pre-packaged
Like Mom's Olde-Time Cookies—
(Eat 'em on the sidewalk,
It's butch, it's democratic)—
I wrote these lines, all interestingly
Worked-over, written-in, cross-hatched,

91

Crossed-out—(but luckily so's
You can see, researchers of
The future, what he put first,
Thought better of, and then, a stroke
Of genius if there ever was, restored)—
And then I tart it up
With 'variants' in several shades
Of coloured ink, quizzical (God, he was such
A private wit!) asides
In pencil, awkward
Blots (how human, how boyish, how)—
Well we can't all be a Shakespear.
(What was the color—*sic*—of his socks?)

Looking over it later,
I find, thanks to you, I've written something, and—
Gee, sorry, bud, but thanks all the same—
Keep it for myself.
Sincerely.

VII

THE LONELY INSOMNIAC

WHILE you enjoy sound sleep,
I the insomniac am deep in light.
My head is full of blazing night
That mocks the vigil I must keep.

I wrap myself in lamps and fires,
And the four walls are a shining jail.
The blinded windows rattle in my pale
Bones, the skeleton that never tires.

The dark is lit as bright as day.
I watch your dreams with open eyes.
The planes are heavy in my hanging skies.
My love's asleep and far away.

THE INSOMNIAC TO THE SLEEPER

YOUR simple sleep
Is mystery.
I cannot fathom
Its open sea.

You drift deep
On the moonlit bed.
Your arms are cast
Around your head.

Your breathing barely
Comes and goes.
I cannot touch
Your strange repose.

I am the clown
Of night, but you
Are its own darling,
Dear and true.

Your face is far,
Your limbs are free.
When will your dream
Awaken me?

THE INSOMNIAC AT DAWN

Now at this early hour that is so late,
I raise the rattling shades
Upon the gardens wet with mist.
The green of leaves and hills parades
Its quiet wildness white with flower.
A bird beats in my wrist,
Faint as the mist's hanging shower.

The washed songs of several birds
Are jets of rain
Fresher than any sleeper's words,
And brighter than my pain.

AFTER THE LIGHTNING

THE rain suddenly stops,
But under the shattered tree
A heavier shower drops.
Warm tears from dead leaf—
A ghost's long memory
Of one persistent grief
That cannot find release
Until the brain's mad thunders cease.

Although the stroke of light
Has killed the wood's deep life,
Leaving its riven night
Defenceless, it is not beyond
All hurt. A longer knife
Shivers each withered frond
With the slow and steady pain
Of a past storm's protracted rain.

PUBLIC HOLIDAY

Rain makes a desert of the summer square
And rakes the street of flags and people,
Leaves the overflowered rosebush bare
And wets one side of the witch-hat steeple.

It plunges heavy hands into the plots
Of cabbages, and rattles rows of beans,
As big as sparrows down the gutter trots
And drums the rhubarb's jungle leaves.

I sit alone and laugh in the dry,
By the open window watch its force
Shatter the long, smug summer day
And spit on the cricket its rapid curse.

Alone in the cool dark room I sit
Away from the fuss that summer makes,
While the smoke from my private cigarette
Snaps at the rain like nettled snakes.

ABSENT SUMMER

ALONE I sit at evening in the sad room
And watch my window darken with the hill
On which we lay one summer afternoon.
Above its dusk, the sky is dying still.

A cloud grinds the glass with rain.
A bird flies; each wing-beat is its last.
The hedges still come close across the lane,
But summer is already in the past.

Wild ponies wander on the hill's long crest
And down the valley where my sleep has fled.
The nightingale has left her thorny nest,
But I watch on until the stars are dead.

The morning star is Venus, the defender
And destroyer of love's famished birds.
I think of life, but find the thought too tender,
And the season too remote, to touch with words.

THE EVIL EYE

I REMEMBER now that killing look
That masked itself with love,
The bleak blue eye in the brown face
That in the sunny courtyard's dim arcade
Glanced off my open book
And in that instant read me to my death.

I know now, devil in disguise,
You are the demon come to spoil the light.
Your moonbright hair shall be your heavy curse;
Your supple lending of a word
Shall cramp your neck in rigid hells.
It is your dead bones that I touch.

I do not forget the sign of the Scales
In which, mock justicer, you came to me.
Now, on the autumn birthday of that death,
An apt pupil, I return full measure
The gathered poison of your glance, my dove,
And kill all dark and thin-faced creatures of your love.

ALL SOULS' MORNING

Love, your sparrows are busking in the crippled tree.
The ground here is dead and creepy as a trodden wreath.
Bad apples knock their skulls together in the clay.
A snail drags glitter-frost along the path's brick verge.
The air tastes sharp as flowers in a pail.

You know this place, though you forget it's here.
The spider's cordage snaps across your face.
A white bloom is on the blunt late rose's buds,
And on the winter cabbage's creased leaves
Dew runs to one big teardrop at my finger's touch.

On this new and every morning of the living dead
I send you my face, that changes hour by hour;
The clown's mug laughs itself away
To the ghost of a look that cannot let me sleep:
Its eyes annihilate you in their pits of clay.

Careless love, that left me lost in hell,
I spit you back your curse, with all my hate.
Now, in this dead dawn, I make our shadows meet,
And fondly wish on you my narrow death,
As long and bitter, and as incomplete.

IT'S MY TURN NOW

UNSCRUPULOUS charmer, I remember how,
When first we were friends,
You talked of others you had known,
And of their different ends.

How all came right, of course,
In the happy end, through love,
And how you could look back on them and smile
At the mad days they are a memory of.

How well, poor fool, I thought I understood
Your meaning then, and willingly commended
The power you used to conquer them;
Yet wondered how they really ended.

I had a feeling that their lesson
Must have been like this:
A raking emptiness that cannot thrive again
On love's abstraction, the rejecting kiss.

Now I seem to hear you talk to them
At gay next meetings, like a song,
Or to the new victims who seek you out
Of the queer fool I was, of 'what went wrong'.

And it will all have been
For the best, really, although
It was tough it had to happen in that way;
And they'll agree with you that it was so.

I can see that one commiserate, and smile,
This one laugh, and the new one listen, rapt and dumb,
As I did, so little understanding
That another's turn could come.

THE PRODIGAL SON

For my father, died 21st January 1958

In a cold season you suddenly left our home
When I was far away, and sick in mind.
Those harsh days in my distracted winter
Must have touched you, too, and the heart
That failed you as my own gave up the ghost.

My dark nights blazed with sleepless candles
In my drugged room shuttered tight against the bells,
The stars, the snow, the people thin as burnt-out sticks,
The black and iron-frosted gardens of a city that was once
A living rose of stone, and now was only stone.

The devil took me there, and spoiled my innocence.
I did not know how pure my heart had been
Till then and there, when that fair-faced demon came
With willing smiles and dangerous embraces
To poison me with kisses, and to take my name.

Out of my flowering mouth he sucked my words,
And from my open hands tugged lines of life.
He made me touch a saint's dead bones
With blind fingers that my thoughts had made unholy;
He took away your spirit from my eyes.

I lent myself to evil, thinking it was truth
Beyond all good and ill, beyond
The neat divisions of the body and the soul.
Father, I saw my long delusion, for the grace
He promised me was vain, and never could be yours.

The trouble gathered in the face you knew,
That always changed, from hour to hour,
But now became a fixing mask of grief, the clown's,
A stunned look I shall never tear away.
The devil made me love his cruel gift.

104

There came that long night of my perjured soul,
The night in which you died, so far away,
As if my absent hell had killed you, too.
In the dead morning, one living thing within me
Was my sadness, that made me dress in black.

I did not know that you were dead,
And yet I dressed in black, to damn the sun
That led my shadow through the rigid town.
I did not know that you were dead,
And yet I bought your flowers, deep carnations.

Father, this was a year of bitter tears.
It seemed I had been weeping always for my fall
From grace, my own sad death, and still
Go weeping with an evil eye, and weep for you
Who left me lost and far away, beyond forgiveness.

I came back, father, to our wintered house,
And saw you lying still and cold and glad,
A mask of mute astonishment upon your face.
I touched your lovely forehead, chill as stones,
And felt beneath my hand the outrage on those other
    bones.

In San Esteban, beneath the altar, still they lie
In broken peace, a peace I killed, a devil's pledge.
—O, father, let my last touch rest your ashes, love,
And from this sleepless desert drive my devil out:
Let you return, and smile upon your prodigal.

PRINTED IN GREAT BRITAIN
AT THE UNIVERSITY PRESS, OXFORD
BY VIVIAN RIDLER
PRINTER TO THE UNIVERSITY